TALE OF THE MAYOR'S SON

Glyn Maxwell was born in 1962 of Welsh parents, and grew up in Welwyn Garden City, Hertfordshire. After reading English at Worcester College, Oxford, he worked in Geneva as a gardener and painter for a year. In 1987 he won a major scholarship to Boston University to work at poetry and playwriting under the guidance of Derek Walcott and George Starbuck.

He now works as a freelance publishing editor and reviews poetry for various publications, including the *Times Literary Supplement, Poetry Review* and *Verse.*

He won 3rd prize in the Poetry Society's National Poetry Competition in 1989, having been commended in 1987. His poems have appeared in many magazines and anthologies. He was the subject of a special author feature in *Agni Review* (USA), and was featured as one of eight 'New British Poets' in *Poetry Review* in 1987.

His first book of poems, *Tale of the Mayor's Son* (Bloodaxe Books, 1990), is a Poetry Book Society Choice.

TALE OF THE
MAYOR'S
SON

GLYN
MAXWELL

BLOODAXE BOOKS

ISBN: 1 85224 098 9

First published 1990 by
Bloodaxe Books Ltd,
P.O. Box 1SN,
Newcastle upon Tyne NE99 1SN.

Bloodaxe Books Ltd acknowledges
the financial assistance of Northern Arts.

Typesetting by Bryan Williamson, Darwen, Lancashire.

Printed in Great Britain by
Billing & Sons Limited, Worcester.

For James & Beth Maxwell

Acknowledgements

Acknowledgements are due to the editors of the following publications in which some of these poems first appeared: *Agni Review* (Boston, USA), *Manhattan Review, Oxford Poetry, P.E.N. International, PN Review, Poetry Book Society Anthology 1988-89* (PBS/Hutchinson, 1988), *Poetry Review, Poetry Wales, Poetry with an Edge* (Bloodaxe Books, 1988), *Stand, Times Literary Supplement* and *Verse*.

'Farm Close', 'I.M. David Penhaligon', 'Mr Harmen to You' and 'Tale of the Mayor's Son' were broadcast on *New Voices* (BBC Radio 3).

'Just Like Us' won 3rd prize in the Poetry Society's 1989 National Poetry Competition; 'Hoodhead' was a prizewinner in the 1989 Bridport Poetry Festival; 'Bonfire' won 2nd prize in a competition run by *Writers' Monthly*; 'Select' took 4th prize in the 1989 Greenwich Poetry Festival.

Contents

My Turn

I have been so enchanted by the girls
who have a hunch, I have been seen

following them to the red and green
see-saws. There have been a few of them

I recognised. I have been recognised.
I have stood on the roundabout and turned.

I have swung, uselessly, not as high as them.
Then seen the parents coming, and the rain

on rusty and unmanned remaining things.
I have calculated west from the light cloud.

Cried myself dry and jumped
back on the roundabout when it had stopped.

Started it again, in the dark wet,
with my foot down, then both my feet on it.

Tale of the Mayor's Son

The Mayor's son had options. One was death,
    and one a black and stylish trilby hat
he wore instead, when thinking this: I Love.

The town was not elaborate. The sky
    was white collisions of no special interest
but look at the Mayor's son, at the bazaar!

'I've seen her once before...' Her name was this:
    Elizabeth. The Mayor's son was eighteen,
his mind older than that but his mouth not.

And had no options. 'Hey, Elizabeth!'
    I could say what was sold in the bazaar,
I could be clearer on the time of day,

I could define Elizabeth. I will:
    Every girl you ever wanted, but
can't have 'cause I want. She was twenty-one.

'Hi, –' the name of the Mayor's son? Anything.
    'Let's get something together!' someone said.
'The Mayor's son out with Lisa!' someone gossiped.

The afternoon, about to be misspent,
    stirred coffee with its three remaining fingers:
'They are sugar-crazy, they are milk-lovers,

and they won't last.' Some things about the town:
    blue-printed in the days of brown and white
and laid down one fine evening, late July.

Musicians lived there; painters; people who
    did murders but deliberated first;
town-councillors for other towns; widows

of chip-eating, soap-using carcasses
    who still watch television on occasions;
ex-famous people too, well one or two,

ex-people, come to think of it; some mates
    of mine, no friends of yours, not you, not me;
a prostitute or two policemen or

a cabbage-patch doll buying a new home;
    a band of Stuart Pretenders; a fire-hose
on motorbikes, frequenting clubs and stuff;

a catholic, a protestant, a bloke;
    insurance clerks, accountants, a red horse
belonging to my cousin, and of course

the man himself. No, strike him, he just left.
    Divide the town into eleven parts,
throw ten of them away, and look at this:

They skated on the ice at the ice-rink,
    Elizabeth and a black-trilbied boy
who kept his hat on. I'd have hated that

had I seen it. I hate people who
    make such alert decisions to impress.
I'd have him on his arse. Oh good, he is.

Elizabeth, white-skirted, – no more clues –
    swooped to pick the Mayor's son off the ice,
and pterodactyl-like he shook himself.

Hat elsewhere, hat kicked on by a small bully
    and ruined by the bully's friend. Once,
that would have shelled and reddened my idea,

to see such fun. But nowadays I just
    cram it in with all the other eggs
for omelette. Skate, skate, you're crap at it,

whatever your name is, you Mayor's son.
    The Mayor's son and Elizabeth, oh my!
The middles of my afternoons in England.

Three simultaneous occurrences:
    a hump, a testimonial, a bomb.
Back to the ice-rink, just in time, we –

– There they are! Their two bicycles propped
   for vandals who'll show up in half an hour,
and off they go towards the library.

Conveniences everywhere, a town
   complete with detail, and the gardens so –
green and, and – and there! This is a poem

of love, but the boy had to urinate
   and did so, while Elizabeth began
to make a Christmas list, and left him out.

The air began to gather, pointilliste,
   and the first lamp went to a sorry pink
that wouldn't last, was a phenomenon.

They crossed roads, Beauty Gloved and the Mayor's Son,
   they made split-second choices that saved lives.
The library was all a welcome cube.

The library was full of walruses.
   Or people who resembled walruses.
Or – no. Let's say: People who would bear

comparisons with walruses, and might
   confess it was a modern poet thing,
post-Tennyson: Irish perhaps, or French.

Outside the library, the skinhead world
   dropped litter, picked up girls, and spat, and wasn't
literate, and walruses, elsewhere,

moaned in the sea and didn't give a fuck.
   So much for images. The library
was full of books. The books were like more books.

Some books were overdue. A man called Smith
   had borrowed Dante's *Purgatorio*
but not the other two. I had them both.

A man called Dorman had a book on trees,
   which nobody had mentioned recently
though it was ages overdue. A girl

who'd stripped the library of Sailing books
   had drowned recently, and was so slow
to answer warnings that they'd phoned her up

to ask politely for their library books.
   A dictionary had gone missing too
but the Mayor's son had other things in mind!

How do we know? We don't, but he had options,
   and watched Elizabeth watching the books
on Archaeology, and calling them

'Unusually specific.' The Mayor's boy
   nodded his head of ordinary hair
and felt Love working with the utensils

he generally called his heart and soul.
   'Well this is it,' she said, 'but it's too short.'
The sky was mauve, no other colour, mauve –

the walruses, the ice-skaters, the books!
   The Mayor himself was coming home to dinner,
and I was splitting up with Alison.

I think it was that day, about half-six.
   The bully, meanwhile, read about a bike
and mentioned it to his pathetic dad

as a potential Christmas present. I –
   sometimes I hope he gets it, sometimes I
devoutly hope it kills him. Anyway,

'The Library is closing now.' The Mayor
   expected his son home. Elizabeth
expected that as well, didn't expect

what happened next as they waited for the cars
   to lose their nerve and stop. He put his hand
behind the head of this Elizabeth

and bruised her with a kiss, a mad one! He
   receded and she reappeared, a girl
with somebody to marry, and not him,

her mouth politicised indignity,
    her eyes becoming tyrants, après-coup:
'How dare you?' What a question. How dare *you*?

Because we don't know what – because we do –
    Irrelevant! Elizabeth was off.
The traffic-lights were either green or red –

it doesn't matter. Look at the Mayor's son,
    no girl, no hat, under the sodium-
lamps of his home town. (Elizabeth

was born here too. Actually, so was I,
    but Alison moved here in '83.)
Change, traffic-lights! Go, hatchbacks of the time,

the buses, and the other cars! Next year
    the Mayor – who now eats veal with his wife
and son, fills a second glass with Soave

and tells a joke, and the son laughs – the Mayor
    will be deposed next year: his son will choose
a university, *it* will say no

to him but take Elizabeth, for Maths
    not Archaeology, and Alison
will suddenly, one day, in a Maths class,

befriend Elizabeth, and find that their
    acquaintances are mutual, like me
and the Mayor's son, and in a stand-up bar

all evening they'll be there. Meanwhile the books
    will pile up in my world, and someone's hat
will find its way to me and I will wear it.

Goldfish
(for Melissa Dobson)

We go down to the harbour
quick, before the rain
with our backpacks and emblems
and shortage of evidence
and in the dark folds of water
we picture the goldfish.
Then the rain, the agreements.
Then the sunlight and goldfish,
the actual goldfish,
      alarming and moving
and the boats out fishing out
      blood. We were mortal
and now we were hungry.

Stairs and Oak

Yes, the standing on the uppermost stair
at four, I think, at night or in years – my folks
would know. The going 'Why.' The being there
and going 'Why.' The grand unreadable books
all around, the stairs down
to a guessed end.

Yes, the owning a name and suddenly
at four in age, that treasure intercepted,
keen to have it told, the Why, the Why...
I'd like to know what answer I expected,
before I got the 'Why?
It has to be

that way.' Then pale absorption of the worst,
a blip in the young brain, after which
all is a green examined quiver, nursed
by kindly terminable patients, and the rich
forget-it of the flushed
young sufferers,

the adolescent shrug of my own shoulders.
Then yes, the lying in another garden
as the hour seeped for the first of my grandfathers
in one of the downstairs rooms. I saw the curtain
gather. I smoked under
our giant oak,

our Charles II oak, I followed its arms
through calm, gradual argument, towards
the smaller points, the versions, the odd forms,
the dead-ends, and a single one towards
a bud on the white sky,
then out, away.

Five-to-four (3.55pm)

Who hasn't ever thought
of all the five-to-fours:
today's and yesterday's,
last Friday's, and your first
ever five-to-four? So

everywhere you've been
they'd be: smoking in shirts,
or trudging in school kit,
or babies in dark rooms,
or they'd be drunk in fields

(perhaps not in your case)
or holding hands? surely,
and there'd be many dozens
crowding the same desk,
populating the woods,

watching for the same
or very different girls;
some driving, some in libraries,
some shaving, some in tears;
all oblivious

of hundreds of the others
at five-to-four. Who hasn't
ever thought that? You haven't?
I'm thinking it now.
And they all turn and stare.

They Lessen One

Coughs. Ash. A corner's dust. The curtain's answer
to that, remarks on any sort of death
and all degradables, you and me both.
Cabbage, horses. Royalty. That dancer.

And finally, down through the smooth decays
to the Atoms, alert and boyish, not
possible but proved. There, nothing but.
There, too busy, too light in their ways

to live in terms of futures or quotations,
they sort, among the balls and pucks they sort
and dodge and are. Me they puzzled, caught
with the least likely of their recreations,

you. And prodded with a girl's impatience
like – here we go again – like they were taught.

Mattering

But the next day I was a hood with teeth,
and the red leaves were ankle-deep. Utter,
gaping memento mori to myself –
Alas! to cherish these things so – bobbing.

And this I memorised: if, in a yard,
you swear you see something, it's nothing but
another guileless chemical moment. –
When the bonfire-smoke mourned into the sky

forgetting murders, I was holding out:
my hands were these accomplishers, but blue,
distressed with what was animal in them

and wouldn't stop its mattering. 'Alas' –
an old word on an old cloud, like my God
when I was frowning at a picture-book.

The Albatross Revolution

I

The Residence was coddled by the light
of albatrosses, many of them silent.

The summerhouse had had a green door then,
which banged and banged and shut, and the relevant

daughters of their Highnesses were to be seen
nowhere – probably putting on a play

or, at that flashpoint of the century,
heading somewhere new, reluctantly.

II

The albatrosses having flown inland,
the green door flew open. The daughters and

the friends they had were two groups that were not
there, and starlings were a small group that was,

though not for long. The lawn was wide and cold
with all these new commotions, and the sea

licked at the bony ankles of the cliff
as if it was their Highnesses. It rained.

III

Somebody laughed hysterically when
the full whiteness of the Residence

exposed itself to all – the random all
who shoved each other out of the forest now.

The starlings jabbed in the orangery.
The albatrosses did something different

elsewhere, the details quite available.
There was some sour cream in the Residence.

IV

There were some bottles in the sea. The cliff
had stood ten centuries of them, and would,

to be honest, stand twenty centuries more.
Men climbed the chimneys of the Residence

even as podgy womenfolk exchanged
recipes involving cheese and sour cream.

And they flew flags, the men. And starling crap
made constellations on the cold wide lawn.

V

It rained. Whatever the flag meant, it sulked
or, at that flashpoint of the afternoon,

resulted in all sorts of things. The cream
was put to its sour use. The Residence

was multi-purpose, snaps of albatrosses
hung all about. The air grew dark and green

as uniforms, and, catapulting out
of a high window, the Albatross-Man.

Flood Before and After

It reeled across the North, to the extent
that even Northerners said 'This is North!'
and what would you have said, to see a sky

threatening the children with great change?
Extraordinary clouds! Spectaculars!
There was the Dimden family, in their barn.

And long, quite vertical rain, the three horizons
hunched, different formulations, browns
and oranges. Then the unlucky Greens

running with their sons to find their sons.
The scarecrow and the crow, they did okay,
getting dark together, but unfrightened.

Fists of clouds! Genii of glamour!
Not to mention thunders, not again!
There stand the Dimdens, safe and sad.

The Greens have found their sons! Now for their daughters.
But out goes the lightning, giant's fork
into a mound of chilli, steaming there

and where's it gone? Into the open mouth,
barn and all, flavours and seasonings!
Cuddle in the rain, old favourites.

There goes a Noah, borrowing a plank.
A little slow to move, we thought. It ends
with tangles, the new rivers, and the sunshine

formally requesting a rainbow. Granted.
The creaking and excusing back to work.
A valuable man was lost in it.

That was in the paper, with the picture.
All the Northern correspondents went
reading to the telephones, all cold,

which brought the dry onlookers from the South,
gaspers, whistlers, an ambassador
and leading lights to mingle with the hurt.

The clouds were diplomats of the same kind,
edging over to exonerate
and praise. And then the royal son arrived,

helicoptered down on a flat field,
glancing up at the sky through the whuz of blades,
attending to the worried with a joke.

Hell, I don't know what -- we were all cold.
The landscape looked an archipelago.
The Dimdens finally twigged, the Greens were found

beating the Blooms at rummy, in a cave.
All were interviewed and had lost all.
All saluted when the helicopter rose.

Only some came up the knoll with us
to check our options. Only two of those
saw, as I did, Noah's tiny boat

scarcely moving on the edge of sight
below the line, and only I'd admit
the crow and the scarecrow were rowing it.

Cottage in Forest

The captains halt, gasping: they left
good hearts, barbecued, in a glade,
and the ash, green and wishful there,
is scuffed by odd infrequent breaths
but gets nowhere. The captains peer
into the cottage, their hands soft
on window-sills, their eyes wide,
and bitter hollows in their mouths.

Then the knock, and then the simmer:
the captains counting the live twigs
on her one table, while her eyes,
white as the spots on deer, avoid
each guess and question. They say Please
and she does more. The air gets dimmer,
grainy, doltish, the roof sags
with rain. The captains go to bed

anywhere: in the unbrushed place,
under the table, by the stove,
on the hard floor beside the bed
they keep for her. The rain lets up:
its epilogues alert the wood
to possibilities of peace.
The cottage shudders with the rough
organic problems of men's sleep

and she is gone to the wet glade.
Nowhere to live, nowhere to rest,
all love involving a slow trick,
all light ever prepared to fail:
but there they are, bulls in the dark,
the captains' hearts! – they are not dead,
only walking carbon, only lost
in wet forests of ash and steel.

Drive to the Seashore

We passed, free citizens, between the gloves
of dark and costly cities, and our eyes
bewildered us with factories. We talked.

Of what? Of the bright dead in the old days,
often of them. Of the great coal-towns, coked
to death with scruffy accents. Of the leaves

whirled to shit again. Of the strikers sacked
and picking out a turkey with their wives.
Of boys crawling downstairs: we talked of those

but did this: drove to where the violet waves
push from the dark, light up, lash out to seize
their opposites, and curse to no effect.

The Pursuit

Running through woods he came to the wrong wood,
the round wood. And he stopped there like a man
would in a sudden temple, and his own blood beat
on the cocked side, his hurt side, his red portside.

Running through trees like a deer, victimised,
a sprinter, of a minority, he passed
on into blacker greens and deep betweens,
lost to sight. We shrugged the Home County shrug.

'Running?' muttered those who report and wait:
'quickly?' added by them with a hunch and pencil:
'and with a scared look?' mentioned by the cadets:
'away?' as was firmly noted by those who are here,

he was seen. The relevant people looked for him,
I know, because their vans were parked on the rim
of the right wood, and they took their torches with them,
and left their maps and their furry animals hanging.

'Running, quickly, away, with a scared look?
Escaping.' The constructed xeroxed faces
appeared on walls from here to the uncrossable
M110, and it was said

the outer elms came back to life when the wire
linked them, to politely counsel 'Don't',
and in the ring of fire the rare and common,
darting, hopping, slithering, trudging, dragging

towards life-leasing coldness, from the smoke,
met in the heart of the wood and stared and were doomed.
It was said in the crack and crackle the stars went out.
The birds alone took life and the news away.

In the dry filth of the aftermath the drivers
found belongings, bagged and took them and waited.
Then radioed superiors on the rim.
But he ran elsewhere, though a red X was him.

The End of the Weekend

The chairs were folded up when the light was,
mid-Sunday afternoon; the poplar trees

prepared to bend, and bent, and stood again
behind these disappointed people, ten

assorted family-members, girls and blokes
spending the day as uncles, sisters, folks,

and now, with the bad summer in its shed,
ten private citizens, reflecting, sad,

the family a name, the drinks all drunk
before the bloomin' rain. No one to thank

now, and the two red cars a mile along
the wide woodside road. No one said nothing

as the group walked, except the husband who,
in finally admitting that he knew,

omitted to tell anyone, except,
later, his youngest, who was tired, had slept,

and wouldn't carry anything. Her brother,
two steps, two years ahead, wouldn't either,

and the slim eldest sister, who was scared
of her exam results, was also bored

and carried the large hamper. The first fork
of lightning shot, split, lit up the whole park!

In what followed, the mother of the three
said she'd been right. No one could disagree.

The thunder came and disappointed all
who wanted this late failure dark and full,

an excuse for hot toast later, and then
much much later, to be remembered-when.

But the half-mile mark came, and with it more
of the same slanting unrelenting pour.

The quiet husband crossed the road (this side
had only a grass verge, no paving.) Odd,

how very slowly and diagonally,
gradually, the rest of his family

did the same thing, waiting for this green truck
to howl up, and slow, as if to look

at the divided, drenched and carrying
people, and then to wrench off, rattling.

At last the move was made. This family
had the name Anderson. No tragedy

had struck. In general, they were content.
They never tried to be a thing they weren't,

and what they were, they didn't think was best
or most important. They belonged and fussed

and voted when they could. The other five,
the as-yet-unmentioned, had the name Love

(no really) – Mrs Love (née Black) was Mrs
Anderson's (née Black's) sister, and this is

her, holding the dark blankets, her coat
as dark, in the now slackening wet.

'Nearly there,' and that was Mr Love,
needlessly consoling, soaked enough

to tell the story, Monday, at the site.
And their one son behind them, fairly bright

and cracking jokes at somebody's expense,
somebody dead now, taking no offence.

That's eight. There was an older Mr Love,
leading from the front, and his new wife

gamely alongside, cheering up the kids.
Another blink of lightning, and the hoods

of dwarfs at the roadside, counting up:
'One, elephant, Two, elephant, Three –' (CLAP!)

cruel over a different town, not theirs.
That's ten. That's all of them. They reached the cars

and as the rain ended, and the green light
air was breathed – it was still not all that late –

they towered themselves in, and some of them
were unseen. None of them was clear. A dim

thunder I could hear, preceded by no
lightning, nothing – no I don't think so –

they drove away. One drove away, then two,
and there was nothing. What those people do

now is everything. I know that now.
Don't tell me different. What they do, how,

under the rains of these bad summers, that
is all that's going to change, going to get

things better, fairer, cured, allowed to grow
on the great field, in the great shops tomorrow

filled with the many selves. And in new rain
the neither-here-nor-there but with a plan

were home by now, I guess, the TV on,
the kettle hushed and boiling, the day gone,

the house perhaps all light. But I don't know,
and when you tell me things you think you know,

don't tell me what they look like, how they sound.
Tell me what kind they are, and how kind.

Just Like Us

It will have to be sunny. It can rain only
when the very plot turns on pain and postponement,
the occasional funeral. Otherwise perfect.

It will have to be happy, at least eventually
though never-ending and never exactly.
Somebody must, at the long-last party,

veer to the side to remember, to focus.
All will always rise to a crisis,
meet to be shot for a magazine Christmas.

It will also be moral: mischief will prosper
on Monday and Thursday and seem successful
but Friday's the truth, apology, whispered

love or secret or utter forgiveness.
It will have to be us, white and faulty,
going about what we go about. Its

dark minorities will *be* minorities,
tiny, noble and gentle, minor
characters in more offbeat stories.

Its favourite couple will appear in our towns,
giving and smiling. Their tune will be known
by all from the lonely to the very young

and whistled and sung. It will all be repeated
once. Its stars will rise and leave,
escaping children, not in love,

and gleam for a while on the walls of girls,
of sarcastic students beyond their joke,
of some old dreadful unhappy bloke.

It will have to be sunny, so these can marry,
so these can gossip and this forgive
and happily live, so if one should die

in this, the tear that lies in credible
English eyes will be sweet, and smart
and be real as blood in the large blue heart

that beats as the credits rise, and the rain
falls to England. You will have to wait
for the sunny, the happy, the wed, the white. In

the mean time this and the garden wet
for the real, who left, or can't forget,
or never meant, or never met.

The Last Dessert

The sixteen guests sat back, applauding,
table opening like a flower:
two were not applauding, one
had said these things in this last hour:

'Yes. You really must admire him.'
'Born in poverty, you know.'
'Would you care to see that pattern.'
'Hasn't it been windy, though.'

'No. I don't know how he does it.'
'Brought up in a slum, that's right.'
'Couldn't put my finger on it.'
'Yes, I'm lucky. Yes, you're right.'

At nine he rose, the uncrowned King
of Bonds and donned his paper hat,
made an elaborate speech of thanks
to them, then they all sang and sat.

But she was scared of the dessert
still to come. It had gone all wrong.
He sang for it, the pale and hearty
sixteen sang loudly along.

She went to fetch it, called and cheered,
she put it in the sink to see:
brown and pink and crumbled like
a failure. She was twenty-three.

'Where's our bloody pudding?' cried
the envy of the made-it-good,
confiding loudly 'Love her really!'
so the sixteen understood.

She was in the kitchen, gazing,
playing with the end-result
of a not-difficult recipe.
It wasn't the ingredients' fault.

Out beyond the double-windows,
square-lit lawns and pitch-dark woods,
hedges full of kinds of hunger,
hungry things becoming foods.

'Long enough!' the King of Bonds
bellowed to his employees.
'Where's the bloody wench gone now?'
'Don't worry,' said a brave one, 'please.'

'I'm not, I'm starving,' muttered the
example to the lowly-born,
striding to the empty kitchen,
readying sarcastic scorn:

'Don't hurry, will you…' In the sink
dessert, disgusting, brown and peach,
reflecting badly. He was angry.
Nothing smiled within his reach

except the guests when he excused her,
said she was extremely tired.
Then they smiled, excusing, shrugging:
no one stared, no one enquired.

Just the empty chair, the name-ring,
guests admiring certain goods.
Just an ordinary woman
shoeless in the seething woods.

Aurora

Aurora wakes without a kiss and it's not
Sunday it's Monday. She looks at what Monday is.
It's a thicket of rain around her place in the city.
So that nobody else can be seen, but then who's expected.

There's mail. It's nothing. It goes out with the old milk.
Aurora's cold is no better, nor is the world
apparently, from the tabloid she leafs as she drinks
water, orange and coffee. She swallows and thinks.

Maybe he will. Maybe the money. Maybe
the rain letting up like on that riverbank once.
Maybe the change of heart. Maybe the morning
starting again and this the explicable dream.

After all that: evident grey reality,
and she walks in her long green coat, at the edge of her own
territory and out into everyone else's
especially his, wherever he is now.

There's lead in the air, and the elements on her menthol
breath are the wrong ones. He did her so many wrongs.
He's miles away but she doesn't know that but you do.
Use it, if on a bench she's suddenly there.

What happens will not help much. Aurora is earning.
Nothing surprises her, not like the riverbank once
when the man in the blue emerged and appeared a gent.
Now it's pouring with men saying 'sorry' and 'innocent'.

Mr Gem

Mr Gem was now full of himself, he had a party.
    He hired help to help in his house and garden.
The sun shone as predicted by eight admirers.
    The combinations of fish and green
On flavoured biscuits made the children's days
    At the far end, which was far to them all right
But for all that a spoiled and conquered corner
    Of Mr Gem's blue garden. This was July.

Mr Gem had reason to be walking
    In impossible slow motion towards them
With a bottle of dusty red and a gleam of green
    White. And he was dead right to be glancing
Terribly slowly right at the line of wives
    Dipping to foods. Mr Gem has earned the
Blurts of what he says when a little far gone.
    A field day indeed for his brows and tongue.

Eighty thousand had voted for him in gardens
    Browner and smaller than this, and in other months.
The franchise had extended to a dead
    Club patrolling the street with a fact or three
Not far from here. A portrait of Mr Gem
    Hangs in houses hereabouts and is crap.
It stays the same age while he gets bigger and iller.
    Meanwhile demi-skies join in a sulky thunder.

Mr Gem has poisoned his red and his white.
    And the rain comes down like I told it, elephant-blue.
It washes the flavours out, it dilutes the poison.
    The children are last inside and not two by two.
I and a billion vote but are not invited.
    If we were here, there'd be no eats for you.
You are safe with a hot white towel, beautiful lady,
    Rich and fresh, next in the telephone queue.

Poem of the Births

I

And so they came to a clearing, where the ground
was a plaza, and the trees not trees
but millions of lights, angles and squares

and the sky, black as a lid, or the end
of a pearl tunnel, pulled them to their knees
and made them citizens, and heard some prayers

for lotteries and silk, answering each
with billions of likenesses, but nothing
bright or valuable or sexual.

II

This, as the long vagabonds teach,
was in the time of the hotels, when clothing
had a slump and crackle, and an angel

danced on every window-sill, or at least
did not look down. And so, with the night clean,
activating what looked like the future,

the thumping of neon, the girls policed
by anybody male, or on the scene,
and usually shrugged off as human nature,

a couple, an ex-husband and a wife,
were taken from their taxi, and their hands
touched, all their belongings following.

III

Inside the doors, all shades of human life
were somewhere else, but here were sudden friends,
aware and smooth and tired of everything

but dancing, waltzing, while the band played dead
for their children's sakes, and the couple,
nondescript except that they were nondescript,

had two glasses of wine, hers white, his red.
They were guests, they weren't ordinary people!
They smiled at food and angels as they sipped,

and the grand ceiling glistened. By eleven,
he was at his mean tango, and her watch
was on the wrist of an appealing prince

who said he had a call to place to Heaven
and vanished suddenly. But something much
more wonderful occurred later on, and since

it has, I might as well tell you that when
the night was over, seven hundred cabs
were waiting for the two of them, and not

one child was born that night but ten,
and all in that hotel: a ring of debs,
two vandals, and that fuming in its cot.

Girl in Films

The girl had the nothing talked out of her,
was given the black hat, and made a star:
new films were made in hours, and she cried

in the executive producer's car
while being driven smiling to the door.
There was an engine and a well inside,

it cost a hundred dollars just to peer
over the edge, far more to wind the tar
up to the surface: when an actor died

the girl talked quietly. Behind the bar
the ample barman taped what he saw
and sold it to the network for a ride

inside some woman's cadillacky fur.
The girl froze up and moved in with the czar,
who'd lace one cup in six with cyanide.

Amassing

Amass, the people-loving government
suddenly said, enough to care for the
forgotten citizens, our friends. It meant
the trees. Also, apparently, the air

and a misleading rain edging between
equally nervy pylons, out of favour.
The kidney-donors raised a million.
Some patients had a Fun Run towards Dover

and, gradually, the money grew. The trees,
in this long interim, grew more extreme
in their views and aspects; their old guess,
sarcastically-guessed, was on the beam,

so when the Members came, accepting thanks
with one hand and amassing with the other,
to tile and plaster banknotes to the barks
and winds, to wax and eulogise the weather,

no atom, not the craziest, was one
jot surprised when sea began to fall,
green mud amass, and best friends in the rain
nudge and run, and patients bang the bell.

How Many Things

Five things are happening, and I see why.
They are happening together, in a town.
They are happening together, in a bulletin

and I see why, and they are all warm things
I mean, occurring in warm rooms and involving
warm-blooded animals in clothes.

Money is not involved, I don't think.
Let me check. Anyway, it wouldn't matter.
Everything costs Money, even Money.

People moan about it, but you can't
uninvent it, can you? Well, you can't.
Money Talks, they say, and while they talk

Money changes hands, talking all the while.
The millionaire says: It's not the Money.
The Money says: It is the millionaire.

The minister approaches, angrily
demanding his agreed capital M.
He's satisfied and does his daily sum.

Now he's far more careful about Money.
He doesn't throw it at the hospitals.
It's not the be-all or indeed the end-all

and he's the Minister of both of those.
Anyway, he's not the millionaire.
I mean, he is, but not the one I mean.

He's sitting back at tables of his friends:
face-filling gents in grey and the spotted ties
with hundreds of their wives. I think you think

I'm about to mention thousands of the homeless,
young or inoperable, and many hopeless
owing to cold and taxes, but I'm not.

For things are going on, and I saw five
in a bulletin, in order, five of them
on television, five things in a row.

Well I was in a warm room myself. Well
tired I was, in my new coat and hood.
And my remote control was on the blink

but this I did see: children in a line,
twelve chosen children, they had all performed
acts of singular bravery, in fires,

by swollen rivers, in uncontrollable
buses, they were beaming at the M-
inister, congratulating them.

I watched the Primest Minister of all,
consoling a black man who'd been a white man
yesterday and couldn't move his hand

to make his point but had it moved for him.
I knew the truth and said it in the room.
I saw about the widow in her home,

out North somewhere. They laid on a bus
to bus photographers and famous faces
nearer her, and they banged on her windows

with sympathetic words and envelopes.
How many things is that? That's three. Oh yes,
the Minister for Saying It Is So

was casting casting-votes all afternoon.
The consequence of this is yet to come,
but a good ten thousand people ought to know

the bubbly's hit the roof in a big home.
And the pantomime ends with a bulletin.
I mean the bulletin ends with a pantomime:

a politician and a weatherman,
a large police-chief and a ten-year-old,
a superstar, a priest and a madame,

(that's two in all) are dressing up and flap
across the stage repeating a catchphrase
which catches in the audience and ends

in shouts and tears, a blowing-up of balloons
and triumph and exhaustion and thanks
for quite a night. The asbestos safety curtain

drops and lifts again, as the bowing cast
bring the house down. CUT. That's all five things.
Five things that happened in the same five minutes

– on television, I mean, or in a single
bulletin. You say the bulletin ended
with a bulletin, but I'd gone out by then.

Once Was, Is Now

Once was a rock, is now a knack, a tin
drum which couldn't wake the standing-up,
a man who yawns and sweeps the bumper crop
of frilly flowers into his hammer hand
    and says 'Nobody can'
and says 'Nobody can play on the grass and sand.'

Once was a road, is now a food, a grey
retreating vicar uses a short word,
so all eleven mark it on a card
and crawl across to where they sell water,
    'as white as your own sky'
and even cheaper rates for bricks of milk and mortar.

Once was a man, is now a sound, a quartz
replica of a marble replica, you
upon a bridge in Italy, yellow-
black and yellow like this year's two seasons,
    diamond-mouths and ear-hearts
strewn over the hills: they say you had your reasons.

Once was a tree, is now a face, the time
is all o'clock at once: asleep all day,
asleep in snow, the bathing beauties fry
and serve right up to the revealing mouth
    twisted in sudden fame:
it's hot, but that's okay, and so they shuffle south.

Once was a stone, is now a name, a city
which never stops or sleeps except to work:
up to his neck under the arches walks
a kind of shadowy rocking soul, too starved
    to turn or show pity:
around a tightening throat no blacker stone is carved.

Select

Film it in London. Put
a girl in it they can't
resist or understand

or have. This is her name,
her number. She does this:
she looks like this, look there,

there. By the long railing,
like that. Insist upon
the sigh, the fidgeting

capitulation. Show
it everywhere but first
show it to me. Now go.

* * *

Oh, heterosexuals,
at banquets, over phones
agreeing, in the lift:

this is her. She is it.
You have your open eyes,
your preferences. She

has laughed about them. She
is opening the soft
boxed selection. What

she chooses is to pause,
acknowledging. She sits.
She eats. Nothing is yours.

Mr Harmen to You

Harmen had kept the mornings to himself
for this reason, and what a good reason.
You can't just throw money at the problem.

I mean, the addict shambles down the street
ten miles or so away, under the flightpath
with his clean needle but the sun comes out.

I mean, our hearts are in the right areas,
where they accumulate
a warm sclerotic fur that keeps us warm,

and Harmen is not unaware of this.
Born to legislate and eat and fly.
Trained to tell who, and never why,

ready for the tax cut.
And in the afternoons, the discussions
and pauses at the usual surnames

occupy Harmen. But tomorrow,
at eleven, with the deal in his pocket,
he'll reach under his desk and see star-devils.

The Islander

I have grown my hedge,
and I love my hedge,
and I have the best lawyers
money can buy.

Look, they are leaning
at the edge of the cornfield
in the heaviest winds
recorded. I

paged them here, my
accounting lawyers, to
measure my hedge
in the afternoon:

there are many many more of them
coming from Headsgate
on the silent rail link.
They'll be here soon.

They understand.
They will all defend
my right to grow hedges.
My enemies

will tremble and curse
and admire my strengths
and talk of me always
and mumble Please.

I'll settle right back
in a great green chair
and point at my hedges
a hundred feet tall.

For I am the Islander.
Waters, lawyers,
dogs and armadas
come when I call.

Death in a Mist

Snaps it shut in the night, the man,
and lets it fall and lets it walk:
it's a good book. It's now the talk
of all of us with mouth to move,
stone to chuck, violence to prove,
it's a good read. The three-armed fan

bats the air above my head:
in this hot country men are proud
to bleed and keen to join the crowd
where voices die and resurrect
as shouts. Sapiens stands erect
and winds his moral from the dead

electrocuted sinner he
had first forgiven, kissed and blessed:
it's in the book. In a gnarled west
I saw it, saw a blacker wind
of birds, on every feather pinned
a human coin. The crew of three

slid a great bolt across that sky
where salmon-grey believing souls
dragged pale converts from the shoals
of children. It's a bloody good
idea, they said. The three men stood
upon the beach and by and by

the one man stood. A slow rain starts.
The profiteers open up
the banks, and flood the only cup
there was for us. In steady rain,
the book, its own transparent stain,
flashes up silhouettes of carts,

of crooked neighbours in a mist,
unmentionable, in their lives,
hanging their heads in fours and fives
and hoping. But they meet the crowd,
books wide open, reading aloud
why death comes now, why feet are kissed.

The Second Sons' Escape

Like silence, second sons are impolite,
and like silence might know great things indeed.
If they could be destroyed we'd know them too.

So, in the village hall on Wednesday night,
the Captain closed the door and took a lead,
he told us this was what we had to do:

we had to destroy second sons at once,
or live a life of gabbling shallowness
'from church to launderette to washing-line!'

Those were the words he used, so, once
the orders had been given, and the Press
duly notified, we drank sweet wine

and looked for second sons outside the door.
We were a funny crew, all optimistic
as hopeless wives, a lot of us *were* wives –

some of us were granddaughters, but more
still were husbands from the south, masochistic
stepfathers: a few would lose their lives

in the struggle, we had to admit that
but what was death to us? Unless of course
you were the prizewinner singled out,

and it's not likely, because you just read that.
Anyway, the nuns lent us their horse
and with a yell of hope we trotted out.

Second sons were everywhere, but hiding.
The Market Square was loud with nobody
but dogs of second sons, already dead,

and elder sisters, nervelessly deciding
to ignore their second brother unless he
gave up his wordless claim upon the bed.

'They're hiding in the churches and hedges!
They're hiding in the copses and crypts!'
Our Captain whirled the night about his hat –

'Second Sons are creeping on the edges
and underscoring words on manuscripts!
It's sabotage! Or something worse than that!'

We found one second son in his own room,
crouching at the door: the rest had fled.
We asked him what he'd done and he said 'Nothing.'

The Captain said 'He must be lying!' Soon,
the room was split. The second son was dead.
We asked him what he'd done and he said nothing.

Our posse wrestled down the wooden stairs
and barbecued outside. A ball of noise
flamed above our plates and backed away,

then light and silence filed between our chairs;
we blinked and stood. We fingered our first boys.
We heard the big guns sounding in the bay.

South-South-East

Into the choosing zone.
I'll call it South-South-East.

I am, and I am glad,
a glint, a beast.

When I lope from the Capital
with a long list in my hand,

some of you will be on it.
I scan it on the orange sand

and I stretch, like the long pig
spotted and hunted. I

admit it all, confess the thing,
face the truth, want it, I

have no choice and make the choice
and, choosing these,

get back where I started from.
Nobody's.

Second Son in Exile

My younger sister arrived in disguise
and was passed off the troopship, smiling

at the helpful captain who held up keys
and jangled them. The sky was like a ceiling

in that region, especially about noon,
the very hour I saw her on the jetty:

you can't persuade me, I said through the pane.
She wiped her lips. We wandered through the city,

always on the brink, almost turning round
at every corner to hear running feet

but, instead, talking. 'Have you lost your mind?'
she cried: 'We'll take you back, we'll leave tonight!'

But she always was the great white liar
and I the scapegoat, charred with honesty,

the poisoned elm, the very, very dear
departed. 'You can almost touch the sky,'

she said. We wandered off the point, the crime.
She said the voyage was a loneliness

unblinking, unrelenting. Her new name
was 'Cynthia', she said it with a hiss:

'It's secret, it's secret!' Then the time was up.
Dust on our lips uncracking in the sun

divided us apart. A cargo ship
was flying the right flag, and she got in,

my younger sister, still holding my hand:
'Don't worry. Make the most. It's only crime

to love like that. Others understand.'
The sea that took her glistened like a lime

cut open, and I shuddered onto land,
where every man knew her departure time

and, in his language,
scratched it on the sand.

Dominion

Only the Cliftons' yacht
on the flat sea, tufting out from that
diminishing green shape, their own island,

trim and private. They see
the hyphen, the mainland, they are halfway
and stay still or clamber. And there's a wind.

The daughters see the wash
that fans towards their island, their long home
with a friendly golden dog, a pool, a path,

and the smoke of cookouts
clears the palm trees. And nobody got hurt,
sad or hungry, or got snubbed or diseased

because the five Cliftons
made millions of deals in sterling. No
beggar, ex-associate, shareholder

or friend drags in the wash,
there giving up or splashing. Nobody
has grudges, nobody chews on the beach

or fingers, or reports.
Only the Cliftons' rise and dip at sea,
heading for the harbour at Saint-Dauphin

to shop or dine. Their style
is lifestyle and their lives are sexlives. Oh,
all the sisters turn into daughters

and into ladies, three
blonde and blowing flags of hair, starboard.
Port: the millionaire. Inside: the wife

whose maiden name is Graves.
Now she's in a yacht, and says, 'My yacht,'
quietly to the porthole, and is calm.

The sea is very calm,
terribly mild, as if the yacht will make it,
which it will, and the crowds at the harbour

bask, and suddenly look
there! – white yacht on a blue floor. Under which
blurting killers count down to a billion

slowly, honestly,
between the old green vertices, deeply
moved by the changes, by the vast births

then smash the surface, break
with hump and slash, and they they gape, float,
aghast in the shallows – floundering out

to see, and disbelieve,
a land-edge, broken Xs, Ns of some
sand-chalets and bashed boats, it's all brown

and nothing's anything.
And in dismal Cliff-Town, the hundred men
huddle and wipe again, and stir the beer.

Hoodhead

Clothed in a rottenness to two women,
albeit a stickler in alarming heat and anyway
smoking, against all air and orders, Mr
Hoodhead, it was him by his tallness, walked
in the enclosed arcade in his tie and shirt.

He could buy either a present or both or neither
as likely as not, and he knew it and near the teenagers
coughed a displeasure that was without doubt or blemish
pleasure, at their new ugliness and unluck.
They called him just what he didn't give. Anyhow,

it was the negative-seventh day of Xmas, the
eighteenth window. He stopped at the Body Shop
to stub his stub, there. He re-lit it at Boots.
It was there, at least by the window of it, he thought
of a dear liquid for girls but didn't buy it.

He leaned in the non-wind, against non-enemies.
The shops were all foil and silver. That was the worst
thing. So he did exactly what he'd expected,
intended, fantasised, rehearsed, filmed.
He was so loaded with cash he had a ball.

Everyone who was no one in the town was there then.
Everyone who'd done nothing to make the world
smoother, tinklier, buzzier, cooler, nicer
to Hoodhead, Hoodhead's dog, and Hoodhead's one
vast investment, was chewing to the tubed

decibel hisses. Everyone was obsessed
with that but him! He then nearly bought a book
for one of the women but veered to the giant clock
and its dangling chimes to survey and disillusion
everyone! You are all and forever the poor!

Then it was light-foot, crow-flies, to the fountain
spurting a false suggested gold for hoodlums
to dip and trawl for bits of money and find them.
Which is what Hoodhead did as he was fucking mad then,
fishing from his thin height with a face of scorn.

Christ he got loads of coins, he ran from the glances
out into other arcades and finally out into
fallen snow. He had bones to pick. He was angry
and saw the intended Christmas on housewives' faces
passing. He wanted to die again and he said so.

Poisonfield

We went to vote in our democracy,
    and saw a poisoned field behind a fence.
Dangerous for children, I think I said,

but those behind me disagreed at once,
    pointing out the great wire that the field had
wound itself in. They asked if I could see.

It's safe, they said. We reached the yellow wood
    where we thought the voting gates would be
but no – there was a map, moving with ants

and my best mate shuddered, lost his melody
    around the gatepost, changed his fingerprints.
There was a black cow and a lightning rod:

voortrekkers in the sky, doing the rounds
    of wagons, holiness, and the brown lid
banging out a song for me and thee.

We tried to vote, and were told to thank God
    we weren't the winged things we could clearly see
eating out of half a poor man's hands.

We thanked. We stopped at a dance-hall for tea,
    discussing politics, and our new friends
we couldn't shake off. Then I think I said

Is it time to move to a vote? And the dance
    failed, the disapproving children heard
apologies that sidled out of me...

* * *

It seems to last forever. In my bed
    I sulk and spoil the paper. Tyranny
is mine. I miss the rallies and events

they organise. I finger my one key,
    and on the poisoned field behind a fence
I grow my children and I grow them bad.

Mild Citizen

Sunday is wringing its discoloured hands.
The elms are rinsed of light and greenness, birds
shit and circle over these charlatans
who haggle in the field. I do my work,
    scotching the short words
I really want, the ragged and berserk,
in favour of a point of view. I lean
into the vertical, out of the murk
which pulls and changes what it didn't say
    and didn't know, but mean,
and I'm ready. Ever younger people play
there or near, as the adult town of men
fills up with us, and yellow yesterday
in its sheets, smells. When it gets late
    I walk, mild citizen
of what's suggested, what's appropriate
because it saves my neck. Only, again,
I see the pale, shock-headed Delegate
emerging from the Chamber, and I hear
    the moaning on the lane,
where the mild citizens keep moving, where
empty musicians play in endless rain.

The High Achievers

Educated in the Humanities,
they headed for the City, their beliefs
implicit in the eyes and arteries
of each, and their sincerity displayed
in notes, in smiles, in sheaves
of decimal etcetera. Made,
they counted themselves free. Those were the hours
of self-belief, and the slow accolade
of pieces clattering into a well.
And then the shrug of powers,
and the millions glutted where they fell
toadstooling into culture. Who knows when
they made their killings during that hot spell:
policemen or flies? An infinity
of animals began
to thrive especially, as when the dull sea,
sick with its fish, was turning them to men.

Breath

Inhaling and inhaling. Think of that pain,
to breathe in light and more and inhale again
without having absorbed or stopped or nodded,
to inspire oneself with this cold, bolted air
though it's impossible and agonising,
        not even fair,

and then to call it freedom, a fresh gulp
and then? – The quiet embarrassment of help
from the nurse or foreigner or bearded fellow
of questionable sex, oh but a gentleman.
But first the breaths, the choices uncircumscribed
        as oxygen.

The job is done. What that leaves are blokes
with iron principles repeating jokes
to the same man at half-past-midnight. Holding
breath at the eyehole. And two at the door:
one starting speeches with *However*, the other
        with *Furthermore*.

The job is done, and then? The days are gone
when the tall boy and the clothed pithead simpleton
worked hours and hours, belonged to unions
and had no options. Something was arranged:
an overnight dismantling of the engines
        and a sign changed,

and now all is miraculously cheap,
and leisure's only bad sport is a sleep
or lightning. Parents know what to teach children.
Television addicts know how to deal
with murderers and the confused. Boys know when
        to screen the appeal.

The air is sweet and full over the Midlands,
fuller than before, and sweet. Woodlands
ruined by the impossible hurricane
spray up again, of course, at no expense,
but the encouraging of the good businessman
        and what he wants

take undebated preference. Obviously.
The living standard ups like mercury
and we get what we need – heat, applause,
murmurs as we pass, not conversations,
the endless sorries of a sheepish enemy,
            girls' devotions,

beaches specially left empty, strokes of luck,
progressive captive audiences, saying Fuck
a tidemark of freedom, and the wide choices
afforded by competitive TV.
A boring, terrifying hour alone
            is a luxury.

Inhale. Call these the gifts and chances. Then,
confess their shape and character. Again
recall them, at a sunny shop or church fair
then blow them out, on the wet road home from
hers. Freedom is all, or everywhere,
            or not freedom.

Inhale. In that is old democracy:
the incenses of a swarmed-towards sea,
the meals and proof and anchormen and the norm,
and all the unacknowledged animals
yet to invent themselves from clothes or hatreds,
            heroes' annuals,

the freed mischievous chomper of his greens,
and the underlining expert of the means.
Keep inhaling, all the scouts and apples too,
all justified aggression, all the mentors
and agitators, and the long unpeopled room
            a Nazi enters.

Keep breathing, for the State is air. The air
is still. The choice is lit. Is what to wear
or if to care. Or is – what to have seen
and kept a secret. At the lost top of breath
there is a pausing, unremarkably a-
            kin to death

but missed, the unwatched and esoteric channel
of what could be done. On that, a ready panel
discusses without pause and without sarcasm
how to assist some who can't lunch or dress,
and nobody sits back and finds that 'touching'
or says 'Nonetheless...'

Mine

Someone lied to someone's friend
and all the lamps went out in a
blackbirdless pit a mile down, and
the thousand men came up. Because
the lamps shook to a clinging end
and lies were nodded on, a band
of citizens paraded the
three colours of a thing that was.

The colours are: a copper-green
(it oxidised itself), magenta,
fluid, medicinal, and slow,
the third one an off-cream cream. That
is something to be fought for. NO:
that word likewise. Strike, citizen.
As per usual, the centre
holds, and argument falls flat.

Someone even died, which made
a case for the word 'Principle',
whereupon the citizens
in favour could cry 'Principle!'
whenever enemies were tense
and friends were armed and/or afraid;
the act itself defensible
in alleyways, in principle.

No one's bloody mineral,
and hardly anybody's luck
but there it is, in the dead glint
of what's forgotten: lines of coal
hard-pencilled under us, dark print
of grandfathers and wars and muck,
a mattress for an animal
marching and pleased with his new soul.

Someone even died, and paid
for having been misled. 'Poor man,
to only think of his own need!'
The cities stretched and shut the towns
of brick and radish hands. For feed,
men shuffled underground, and laid
some planks. A filthy trolley ran.
Elsewhere, talk of a billion pounds.

The colours are: a promise, an
obedience and, finally,
a helplessness. Why show surprise?
A century below us, that
would hardly open ladies' eyes
and anyway, a countryman
is only that. And certainly,
a human is no more than that.

I.M. David Penhaligon

His very name a small peninsula
where people greet and pass the time of day
as if it was their time, not London's time,

he would stand and disarm
the regiment of furious old Coles;
the pleasers and the up-and-coming men

he irritated with a victim's question.
They said he had a sense of fun. He had
a sense of human life, a sense of light,

and his old picturesque and ruined shire
was richer than my own,
where lawns are trimmed, and mild intelligent sons

mention the past, and plan the bright to-come.
For him, this Cornishman,
no such accident. Only a memory

warm enough to keep his Party in,
although the other Parties fought it hard.
Only the memory of someone different,

someone who served all his constituents,
however they dressed or voted. He served them,
he stood out. Rising Star and Self-Made Man

will bicker on in the high-ceilinged rooms,
keeping up the game, the snug illusion
of democracy, but – here was someone

worth the honour. The shires will teach
and wither and still teach
the courtesies and sides to every question,

while fists hammer on stereos, and bombs
blow dully in the rain in capitals.
And diehards wonder why.

Remember him, devoted to strangers:
and that a laugh is not a joke on law,
but life itself. And when

the Principle is stated, not discussed,
and the Order screamed – the silence following
is when he would have spoken, and we must.

London from My Window

Cosy in their offices, though disobedient
for tiny little moments before and after
reminders and orders, him and him and her
fax and xerox, apologise, want.

One of three possible, capitalised
oblongs of headline inhabit, noisily,
fronts of good brains, and individually
interest them, but, unmemorised,

self-file backwards, a spiralling deck
into a backdrop to be what was then.
Meanwhile the royallest women and men,
for a dutiful, obligatory wait-a-sec,

occupy hearts and somewhere a single
what-luck citizen, occupied, a day
made. Guarded, walled, with one eye
staring and blithe to the sniper's angle,

the leader of all this, thick with truth,
moves in his or her off-white infalli-
bility, telling, with a home in the tele-
vision, -phone-in, -printer, -graph,

-communications industry. I
bag my space in enormous hurtling
hyphens zooming from A to B, nothing
strange in the window, no mood, no sky,

no question but dumb connection to C.
The news is good. And the news is bad.
And the truth is this. And the point is that.
And the name, address, acts and salary

appear and brighten, green from a tiny,
odder-than-tiny, divide by a million,
and that by a million, and that by another one,
chip. And eyes, once alarmed with money,

are amused by kindness, bothered with peace
but have it, a calm superlative Z
of hush and comfort, where what gets said
is 'Sure' 'Will do' 'Leave it to us'.

But the cumulonimbus northern No
greys and shudders. The western We
slopes to a slicked-back, cream-edged sea
and the Old are huge and long winds blow

the Other, the Different, the Bright Unsure
in, in its swing and accidental love
before the viewer, the voter, the staff,
it's the wild wine-offering good-time Or

for the rest of this day, why not, and his friends
freewheeling home, kind and unobeying
in three o'clock rain, and the very trees swinging
in time and indifference that means, that mends.

Wasp

We were all strained with the food when look, a wasp
was and saw what it smelt on our white table
that damnably good summer: it saw the best

thing for now. The bee was near but wiser,
off engineering better from her own
mauve flowers in a basket off the hot wall:

she didn't want what we had wanted and had,
our spoils and fluids. The wasp rose out and passed
from salad to salad, amazed I suppose with how many

there were to approach and envisage. You,
suddenly poised, with a weapon
lightly awaiting, waited. And when I looked

you all had coshes and swatters and so did I.
The nasty little guy
chose to buzz our heads and would die because

of what it wanted and was.
We enjoyed that animal pause in our long lunch,
armed, mates in sweat and our local luck.

We got it. Who got it? I got it,
and dissuaded the boys from keeping it
frizzing in a jar forever and ever. I crushed it.

Well, I thought, as the bee moved off to tell –
but heavily, bored with its maddening cousins – well:
don't fuck with us, little guys. We're mad as hell.

In the Gap

The road is dark and wet and red.
I never went. I never was.
It was an insult, what was said,
and you shall bleed for it, because
I am the stranger up ahead...

And beyond him, the winter-lights
of freezing inner England, new
medallions and satellites
bejewelling a lucky few
and something being put to rights

elsewhere and very quickly. We
have heard of it, are watching it,
are doing it. The comedy
is nervous, gets away with it.
Cosy with astrology,

though puzzled by the power-lines
and isobars, we gulp and sing
O Little Town, Oh well...the wines
divulge and nod. We'll have a King.
There may be storms. We know the signs.

The field is overturned and wild.
We married in a city, or,
we didn't, but we had a child
or two, had two affairs, or four.
Where was I when that stranger dialled

nine, nine, o-seven, two?
Was I there? The jealousy
of evenings was mine, a blue
and doubtful look, and suddenly
I am the stranger. Words are few.

Infantile, the Government
sits concentrating, deaf, cruel.
It said it went. It never went.
It sat for life. It crushed for fuel.
Its methods were no different.

Another incident elsewhere
on London's wire. On Liverpool's
brick there is a human hair.
Same time, same reason. Rules are rules,
blindfolded, neither here nor there.

The factory is breathing. You
are laughing down a motorway.
Gentlemen make time for you.
Enterprise is underway.
Gentlemen are under you.

All the streets, and all the skies
are dark, and wet, and red. All the
money spent is in your eyes
and mine are spluttering at a
sou'-westerly. And now it dies.

Look: villagers on Pylon Hill,
they sit where the revengers sit.
It does no good. The same eyes fill.
Angels? No, the English. Shit.
Go where the blind orphans drill,

left, right, halt. The glass
is squashed and spilling with its men
so pleasantly surprised. A class
of ordinary citizen
will pay for this. The lorries pass.

And further off, the sentinels
of frozen markets, the dim crews
of high achievers, and the smells
of what had been opposing views.
Of what had been the criminals.

And yes, the kind and cowardly,
the finally blinking 'I believe',
superfluous remorse, the sea,
no tears, a pulling at my sleeve:
a kinder coward next to me.

Perhaps another Saturday
or two. (It's you. We walk. I love
the light up here.) The road is grey
and driven on. The sky above
is fixed and dark. The field is hay.

And the first village comes, a chap
too numb and sly to worry much
and the sky sheets, and in the gap
we drop our knives and our knees touch.
Thunder. Catch my eyes. Get up.

Did I Imagine That

A man in a suit in a field.

Well now we'll start. The lights are red, they blurt
'No Apologies' at the twelve cars. 'No!
Never go!' But the twelve drivers lean,

husbands, mainly, in expensive shirts:
uncontradictable, just waiting, men.
The quietest car zooms at the tink of amber,

and twenty-four are gone before the green
onto the unclogged arterial.
The light stays green. It changes as you come.

Another place, under the very same
vast impending cloud: a gross of boys:
a whole school-year for once together, out

running by a dreary boating lake.
Running the traditional long race.
All of them in grey or school maroon.

The blond one will probably be first.
He's got the legs. The one in N.H. specs
is enthusiastic but wheezing. Tough.

Over the lake, the wind-equipped women,
the dog-walkers, all five of them in brown,
ignore the wind and the curved motorway,

they concentrate on walking and their dogs.
Some may be the mothers of the boys
over the lake, and wondering which boys.

From here, the year, the line of straggling sons
is hardly moving, in its dim games kit,
from lonely likely winner to the last,

walking it. Well – this is the English hush.
Total silence except the motorway.
Driving, running, walking past a fence

one afternoon one month. But something else.
Perceptible slowing of the slow lane:
distraction of the distance runner: gape

of woman: shrug of dog: cloud letting rain:
the moment of the talking-point before
the talking. Then the rain, and the resumption.

A man in a suit in a field.

The Loyal

The next division of perfected men
was the eleventh, and they hurled a flag
in the air's faithful oblong, which, again,
was bed and safety-net and showman. These
    were the loyal. A rag
of ill, unchosen colours, enemies
or minor allies, differences in looks,
rippled at an outpost, in a breeze
of yesterday's malarial undead,
    and horseflies in the nooks
of continents were not the loyal. Said
Witnesses: Such are the Fruits of This.
And so they were. And of the fight a shed
full of soldiers, still politenesses
    between their Was and Is.
Loyal indeed are apples to a yes,
are animals to smells, are regulars
to Old and Tried and what it takes to press
the newly-found disloyal to the Square
    under the tricolours
to answer questions neither hard nor fair.

Officer

The apparatus of the officer
was so well polished you could see your face
apologising in his shield. Or rather,
her shield. Yes, difficult to suss
the difference nowadays,
but that's what happens with the principles
one dresses in a mask to honour. Yes,
the sun caught it at 10.15, a bus
droned it out of sight a moment, then
the boys had to confess
the hands were theirs, and everything, again,
cooled into its twin dead – No, and Not-No –
against which one is useless as the pen
that wrote this, or the Bible, or Hamlet
or Godot

Two Old Ones Did It

Is coped with, skyscrapers and is coped with
yes and blue hands on his slightly duff heart
        get him about.
Is seen with, she a crackpot, yes seen with
and her toy bible all these wires apart
        and bedtime pout.

Try not to, met in an upended hotel
room one century, ordered one baby
        who never came.
Try hard to, vertical, horizontal
did prise, surprise, did say maybe
        and was the same.

Year of the, his idea, and a winding
of one o'clock, a country where, a cold
        quieter than.
Years by the, she remember, grey anything
in a locked room near the Atlantic. Sold.
        Aloner than.

Absent stanza, nothing to report, but:
no really nothing, he nor she, and yet:
        I'm sorry for.
Shouldn't have said, have lots to learn me but:
no really, don't know what came over, yet:
        there is some more.

Found her, he in his coffee-time, relieved
himself to find her, though she mad as a.
        Was recognised.
In France found her this was, and she believed
herself to be Joan Of. Mmm, mad as a.
        He realised.

Anyway loved her, old, dud, on the mend
in the bay window, in the light of was
        both anyhow.
Anyway smiles for something in the end,
to cope with, me to cope with it, because
        both quite dead now.

Hyphen

That the third digit
of the year I live in
will never be 7,
will never be 6,

occurs to me this
lengthening Friday,
makes me think of
tomorrow and someone –

The second digit
will be a dark 9
then a clear 0.
The first digit

has always been 1,
will always be 2,
makes me think of
tomorrow and someone

adding a year
to the end of a hyphen, then
breaking for lunch
in the brilliant sunshine.

Blacksong

All the objects coloured black
are holes: the rubbish-bag, the big
half-burnt thing, the next cadillac,
the wicks, the edges of the rug.
And once inside I own a stick

and clatter it from top to side.
The red objects are then the things
such as the sun and meals. I pride
myself in recollecting songs
of that time. Like the Blumenlied

and the Sweet Chariot. The green
plenties are to lie on while
July the gangster mows the lawn:
by my tight-shut eyes and smile
he knows I'm numbering again

and likes me correspondingly
the less. The objects coloured pink
have been believed elsewhere. For me
it isn't something you can think,
it's something you can do. Only,

the smoke is ogling from the heap
my neighbour made, and I hate that.
The objects with a changing shape
are men delivering a note.
I'll have to cultivate a creep

during the short afternoons
of the nineties. Times changin', or
changed already, but our plans
are probably decided. Her
wrinkling, my hard evidence,

will both be factors. Limousines
will scale the mountains, sniff the air,
assemble into smithereens
and sell for minutes. Anywhere
you look, marvellous girls in jeans

and corsets, marmalade and black
and holey – that's the subject, the
verbs are 'accumulate' and 'lick',
the object's 'in a later blur'
and that's the sentence. Have a stick,

monsieur, be one of a low swarm
of operatives in the grounds
of Mrs Sabel's castle: drum,
tickle, hush. What depends
on this inspection? More, the same.

All the objects, all the summers,
all the ratings, all the cures,
all the throat-clearing of famous
actresses, all the desires
to be the next one, or the same as

that one, all that you can eat
and when you want it, whom you kissed
and when you knew it, all the smart
and lucky form the simple list
of the year Nineteen Eighty-Eight,

though all those zeroes in the figure
coming hint a bob or two,
and all the objects getting bigger,
recentlier, branded new,
are more than holes, they're plots. Dig a

lilac garden, Mr Jones,
servant of, professor of,
supplier to. Rhyme with Bones.
Do nothing otherwise. Make love,
be careful. Dip, and marry once:

dig a lilac garden soon,
in Mrs Sabel's empty fields.
She smooths out in her limousine,
her lime-green limousine. Its wheels
beseem. July has been and done

his time for drugs. He's in the black
elaborate Victorian
October Room. She's coming back,
she's dusting off a citizen
for his own good. The almanack

is open on an amber page
and Mrs Sabel jotted down
my number, my address, my age,
my size. The gods are on the lawn,
gardening: they are cold and huge

and heard the quarrels up above,
when Mrs Sabel founded her
School for Schoolgirls: something gave
on Guy Fawkes' Night: the newspaper
caught fire correctly, like a leaf

or Mr Jones. Back in the town
the objects were all coloured white
except her gown, and the post man,
cock-robin's first mistake, and night.
The porch of Number 17

St Abel Street is washed with light
and children who have seen the film
that makes their mother cry tonight
a million times. In the wet elm
the lamp hangs for the prostitute

she really is, though all the town
is hanging things for Christmas. Whole
families are marching down
to St Dog Square. The sky's a coal
of constellations, and the one

moon, our lone distracted rock
that shrugs around this lump of sea,
is in the wrong, and new, and black.
Say the word Eternity.
Say the words New Cadillac:

between these things, the objects are
magenta, peach, ultramarine,
hog-brown, man-anything, blue pear
in Jones's special Christmas tin,
and lambs in Mrs Sabel's hair,

and Avril, in the East Side bars,
is mixing drinks for regulars
while cardinals and movie-stars
prepare to meet. Binoculars
are lifted by baboons in cars

and the news rings the telephones
of Mrs Sabel. City life,
its plans important. Mr Jones
practically has a wife
and certainly a future: loans.

February: on the lawn
the gardeners have left, a lonely
rake stands up and then falls down
for nothing. And it's cold, it's only
February. Near the town,

even the hands are changing hands
it's so chilly. The conifers
that line the road make their demands,
forgetting their inferiors
will soon be the same colour. Friends

clop by on horses. Suddenly,
all the objects in the room
go crimson and are still. And we
have done this many times. I am
the expert, she the company,

and nothing is intended. So.
She has a schedule. I've a car.
I met her all those weeks ago.
She paints: you see how these things are.
Her name? Miss Sabel. Mine you know.

Today's a bright and quiet day,
and all the objects coloured blue
belong to nobody. The sky
makes sure of that. Where I am 'you'
it may be different, it may,

but black, I think, would be the same,
and all its troops expressionless,
the gap between my time and name,
and writing this, and writing this,
all meaning nothing more than Am.

Us and Nell and Ben

You wishing thing! Across the fields
towards the town go Nell and Ben.
She's in her trouser-suit and gloves,
he's the dimliest-lit of men.

This is the light corner, though, where
McAndale Street and Wytham Rise
meet, down in the breakfast-hall where
you grow sleep in your two eyes

and order. I am on my way
with satchel, bulb and evidence
that what you love can be the way
it goes, and the coincidence

of this – is a coincidence
this sudden meeting in the smoke
so calm and very early on
today. Nor is my joke a joke,

nor are my topics mine to choose:
I wrote them down on a green page,
on a green page, because I heard
how you could dance at a green age.

Now it commences, the long talk.
It feels its way. Far into town
new likelihoods and tributes come
and afternoon in a fine brown.

Superstitious, towards dusk,
coincidences over, we
remain, believers in the dusk,
a two, aware of One and Three

the wishing things. By open gates
into the town come Nell and Ben,
she's in her gloves and eyeless shades,
he's the dimliest-lit of men.

Cressida

I got her. I'd been reading Chaucer's *Troilus*.
I lost her, and was young, and made the connection;
I grew up quickly then,
in that rose pain, despair and gossip, that fall.

There followed the adult months of calm and disgust.
The beers with rivals, sympathetic, the car-seats
to stare at a dull North London
from, to have held and dropped, to have got to here.

Deservedly I had had the best there is.
Deservedly I'd lost it. What remained
is that the best there is
is perfect, gold, brief, or was brief that time.

Now in the decade, I hear of her and we lunch.
The love is unkillable. I will go first.
It is brightness, pride,
and unstainable gold, the collector's one coin

I stare at, and value, and keep, and can do not a
thing with – but remember and compare.
Oh, you could be as good as they get,
dear of the city, but you aren't her, weren't there.

A White Car

To know this is, to know the last one
wasn't this, and to drive towards her
hidden, leafed address, remembering

these: the first one, then the kindest
who remained kind and painting, to
recall the one with arms akimbo

threatening, with little on: these
group and hedge and agree in your knowing,
they know it too, and laugh or shrug

to watch you park a white car smiling.
To wander up the path dead certain
of every small thing being and ending

at that address; to ring a doorbell
unfamiliar, then familiar, to
kiss and kiss and kiss – there is

a large and amicable lifting of glasses
and explaining food, a crowded reception
in all rooms that your duet isn't,

all knowing you'll enter, join, forget
and eat. But never mind how they laugh,
the moody soldiers and the snappy teens:

yours is the last if not the longer
when this one comes, when this one means it
at the top of the stairs, and your short breath

blows all their laughter to what it is,
a loud sadness.

A Whitsun

One of the very first
reasons for what
they would term their love
would have been the green wet
of a late afternoon of
truancy, cloudburst.

Having run they'd breathe
and wonder whether
the hoped and unhoped-for
would stumble together
now, unlooked for
but felt beneath.

And kitchen chairs scrape
an obvious answer
loudly together:
an in-joke, a glance, a
biscuit, another,
a favourite tape

and their quiet eyes
to the window, where
the fostering things –
the rain in the air,
the remembered songs,
the light – would uprise

over the town in their
guaranteeing it.
Meanwhile the adamant
aftermath of what
was a kiss – which meant
the beginning for her –

meant it to him:
a phoning October,
a pairing for shelter
and diaries. Neither
would suffer that winter
or forget that time

but this was the difference,
among the very first
subjects they talked of
and almost the last:
she'd never tire of
hot sun – his preference

was the lucky white breath
of a freezing day,
and a pub, its gleam,
its fire. Anyway,
Whitsun came
with the patterned cloth

creased on the grass
and the ambushing first
wasps, and their moods
outstretched and burst –
they spoke at odds.
The dispersing class

dispersed them, yawning,
he to his suffering
June but free, she to her calm
and turned head sleeping
on a lotioned arm
any brilliant morning.

Actress-As-Cat

I loved Actress-As-Cat.
And if you'd seen her ordering the special
and hoping to enjoy it, or thinking back
and trying to remember my old friends,
    or if you'd seen her look

    and offer you a light,
or known her middle name and laughed at it,
you wouldn't say I was confessing things,
you'd say 'Of course. Doesn't everyone.'
    You'd say 'Get out. Get out,

    you love Actress-As-Cat!
No, *I* don't love her, no, but I don't love.
Get out!' you'd say. There'd be no mystery.
I'd know your jealousy. I'd see your car
    in town but know the truth:

    You lost Actress-As-Cat.
You did that, did that, while I'm the one
smiling at ten o'clock, not telling which
ten o'clock, but telling her alone.
    And then elevenses.

    I love Actress-As-Cat.
You never had a hope, or if you did
it's all you had, and she prefers her meals
with gentlemen like me. Yes, I believe
    I was the kind of man

    made for Actress-As-Cat,
the kind she meant when she turned and looked down
along the Downs that Sunday afternoon
and was sorry. I mean she really was.
    We drove back in the car,

    Actress-As-Cat and me.
You'd have been quiet too, to see her eyes
run clean out of depth, all bright and reading
my poem and praising it. And her hands hers.
    And her soft new word: *his*.

Bonfire

The nests dropped out of the trees, the
dry leaves stirred and gathered them. Bonfire
to bonfire the day raced us.

England's blue stink got behind my eyes.
Be more specific. England's blue stink,
exhaled, made a day to remember.

And she watched, she jiggled in the
savoury smoke. I fell, utterly, in love.

Be more specific. The nests leapt into
the trees. A life-sized moon ushered in
her first words:

'Five: Never forget to wrap up warm.'
Her clothes adored me but she just smiled.
We moved,

on and on, saw the mothers in the bright
windows with the clean dry mud outside, and,
bonfire to bonfire,

the night knelt down, beating the black
trees from our frozen English hands. *Be
more specific.* Her cold hands, my warm hands.

Poem for a Wedding

I had a sunlight poem and a cloud poem.
I'll settle for this meeting of the two,

at this meeting of two, at this beginning
of years of sunlit time, and some cloud time.

It's sunny as I write this, months ago,
imagining these minutes on this tenth

of June, which has a ring to it, or two.
Many of us, at the bright familiar moment,

will say this date in answer to a question
asked in curiosity by one

puzzling at a photograph, from which
we are smiling, out of fashion – he or she

is not yet breathing. Miracles will happen.
The answer is 'the Tenth of June', which starts

the great speech with quotation marks, these two,
who entered this room with a family,

and leave with a second ringing in their ears.
This is Man's best speech, and outlasts years,

with all the best jokes, and the pregnant pauses,
the quiet point that bursts into a laughter,

the moment's sad reflection on what was
a good time, then the good time still to come:

champagne, applause, the whiteness and the songs,
sung for once, at last, on both sides now,

by the intelligent ones and the good-looking
not in competition. It's as well

to remember, in a whole churchful of actors,
singers, storytellers, dreamers, dancers,

amateurs, as in 'lovers of what they do',
that what we witness, and are witness to,

is neither a performance nor a dream.
But, like the best of all performances,

it leaves us sitting, thinking only Yes,
and, like the best of dreams, it's come true.

Dusk

Glad I remembered.
What was prepared for me
and never bettered
was done for me, specially.
Glad I remembered.

Shut my mutinous
mind and enjoyed it,
the suntrap, the mouthful.
The Marlboro, the sunset.
Shut my mutinous

eyes…No. I
refuse to be tired, to
see the light line on my
curtains, light on two
eyes. No, I

play past eleven.
Football, Catch Me,
Murder in the Dark,
Fainites! Watch me
play past eleven!

Spoilsport.
Me, I know a game of forfeits.
Look at all those mayflies,
blueflies.
Spoilsport.

Watch.
Lights. Meet my eye.
With a daughter's red, poising ash
or the luminous green henge of my
watch

falling away,
as if I floated over a site
of act or prayer, on a never-believed
night, and they looked at inexplicable light
falling away.

Mandate on an Eighth of May

There came a mandate for a street-parade.
On Optington Lane, which my good friend S
called Pessington for obvious reasons.

And I called it neither, not living there.
There came a mandate for a street-parade
on George the Eighth of May, and Mrs Bain

rose to the occasion, vase in hand,
to celebrate the celebration of
the very good things that were happening

all over Optington, which my partner J
did not approve of, and she kissed me hard.
Which was a different good thing happening,

which would have happened anyway, without
the flags and ticker-tape and elderly
and large endorsers of the government.

Whose victory was Optington Lane's
victory! By which I mean the sun
was really out and the sky really blue –

down in that shine the wine was sipped, the nine
kinds of sandwiches were sampled, Mrs
Bain practised her speech on herself, Mrs

Applechooser waited for a sign from
the neighbour, whom she loved, and Dr Pools
strolled between the tables with his beard.

When I say street-parade I mean street-party.
That nothing moved in step, neither towards
St Palmer's Church nor down to the Drill Hall

but gathered round about seventy tables
(not counting chairs) and each covered in white
and, as Major Crammer put it, 'Eats'.

My correspondent F put it like this:
'If you can't beat 'em, wait until they croak.
Then you can laugh at them.' My partner J

isn't keen on that, and nor am I.
'Better to laugh at them and drink their wine,'
she said, and kissed me hard, and drank my wine.

All of which explains why she and I
(the love between which can't be that. Explained,
I mean) stood our green ground among the guests

although we didn't live there, or agree.
On certain things – fashion, the occult, God –
not even with each other. 'I agree,'

Miss Partofit was overheard to say
to Dr Pools and the new neighbour's wife,
'This is a moral victory for us.'

'Sweeping up the tide,' said Mr Bain.
'Making the only choice,' agreed the wife.
'Hanging is too good,' ventured a tall

pillar of the local cricket club.
My partner J was circling the tables,
mixing up the wines to make rosés,

and then swapping addresses with an old
donor who said 'Ah, your eyes are brown...'
To which she answered, 'Take this number down.'

And I confined myself to making notes
and placing sandwiches in people's bags.
And writing to a mentor, W,

to say 'We are both well, the world and I.
J has made it what it could be worth.
F reports on it, and S stays sad.

And I would call it Optington, despite
the never-ending news from Whitepool Town
and Roxeter, the illnesses and blame,

the poverty and closures north of here
and west of here and east, despite the rumours
surrounding what occurred at Linsaydown,

despite the hundred dead off the white coast.
Despite the thousand missing now in Thaza.
Despite the million said to have been seen

in Ghad, and the one running after them.
And the long line between Black and Notblack.
And the Presidents waving inside their skins.

Despite the day or night the telephone brings
the cut, and I sit down and need a hand
and brandies, I will call it Optington

and when the jolly sights of Optington Lane's
big big day have been cleared away and swept,
and the flags hanging in the elms look wrong,

and Mrs Bain is very much alone,
and it is really night, I will tell you, you
W who knows it anyway:

we never stole from Optington. My J
knew too much to do that. We never told
a single fat and sipping soul that all

their celebrations made us want to cry
for them. We stole away, remembered as
two strangers who belonged to someone else.'

We did, and then we drank our own concoction
on George the Eighth of May in Optington.
Watching the motorway, watching the cars

of strangers. Watching the stars, or two of them.
It had got cloudy. 'It hurts,' one of us said.
'It hurts, and then it stops,' the other said.

Together, on the bridge, in Optington
on Earth – a real place, not one of my
inventions – we were quiet, it was late:

see us. Remember us. Remember the date.

Tale of a Chocolate Egg

I

The advertising of the chocolate egg
began that day. The slogan was so short
it was the chocolate egg and only that.

The chocolate egg alone on a silk surround.
A little cream-filled general in bed
was what I thought of when I saw it, but

I hadn't seen it yet, and play no part.
The advertising was quite marvellous.
I even saw a lad discard his Mars

in open-mouthing awe at the vast ad.
It was enormous, a whole building's wall!
The walls of a whole block! The chocolate egg

alone in bed, its slogan, as I said,
itself. Look, like this: *O*. But obviously
magnified a million more times.

You couldn't see its centre, it was whole
and flawless, like a real egg. It *was*
a real egg, or representation of

a real egg, or a real chocolate egg.
You couldn't see what came inside it, but,
you could guess it would delight and ooze.

It would, it would be yellow with some white,
a real egg, as we observed earlier.
And children gathered, hoping, under it.

II

Irrelevant and independent, warm
in recently-washed sheets, the brown-haired bloke
awoke. He was hungry and hungover:

he'd been peripheral at an all-niter.
The last thing he remembered was the blonde
asking him not to dance. There'd been a game

in which one told the truth. He'd told a lie
and nobody had been surprised. The blonde
had somehow won. That was a different blonde.

The brown-haired bloke felt dizzy at the window,
a first-floor window, over the east of town.
A massive dirty town. London, in fact.

He saw the houses of about a half
million. He lived on a small hill.
He saw a dozen people on the streets.

'All those people...' sighed the boy whose hair
was the most ordinary possible.
Brown, neat when combed, a normal length,

not all that clean. 'People without names...'
he postulated, wrongly, falling back
across the bed, with nothing else to say.

He checked his Rockwatch. It was Saturday.
He stretched his arms, or sang, or scratched his legs.
Then thought of breakfast. Bacon, maybe eggs.

III

In the corner of the last corner shop
there served an Indian girl. She watched the door.
(Her parents were out back, watching the back door

for more deliveries.) A skinhead came.
'Twenny B'n'H, a pack o'reds,
some baccy an' a Sun, sweet'art,' he said,

chewing, sniffing, glancing at the goods.
The Indian girl sold them, and he paid,
and, as he made to leave, he had a thought.

It was a short and vital thought. It came
sharply to his mind, and it got said.
'Also, sweet'art. I'll have a chocko egg.'

He had it. There were hundreds on the streets!
(People) it was Saturday, the sky
was dry, allowing white, this was a time

of celebration in the banks and pubs:
they'd just confirmed the four-percent decline
in non-violent crime, and wedding bells

had sounded in the new soap, *Cul-de-Sac*!
Flinzi's pic was everywhere from ELLE
to MLLE, via the *Sunday Times*,

and in the clean hands of the brown-haired bloke
though he just read it for the horoscope.
It said he would be lucky. He looked up.

IV

The sun was on its way from I to J,
as it were, way up there, London's own.
The skinhead sat down by the marketplace

and coughed and smoked, and read his newspaper.
He turned a page and 'Cor!' he said aloud,
then turning to the middle, a young man,

he carried on with being unaware
of being watched by constables and there,
in the sunshine, his ex-girlfriend, Clare.

And in his bag his chocolate purchase warmed.
A family nearby had seen the ad,
the egg, and they began admiring it.

The children were young children, and, as if
they'd just been told that, started to complain:
'I want one.' 'I want two.' 'We want two

each.' The egg itself, its sun-gloss brown
underlining its fine quality,
luxuriated silkily, and sold

– to the family, standing in the last
corner shop, and buying 'Six eggs, please.'
The Indian girl was reaching for the best

fresh farm produce, when a small voice said:
'Not those white ones, Daddy, we want these!'
They got them. And the shop-girl watched them leave.

V

Down in the Dwelling of the Brown-Haired Bloke
the brown-haired bloke was hungry. In his fridge,
cool absences and gaps made him a fool:

no milk, no bread. At least not in his section.
Lindsay's shelf had bacon, milk and juice,
croissants, all necessary breakfast things,

while Oliver's, of course, was mainly beer
and the odd onion bhaji. As for his,
pâté and a lemon, and a sole

hopeful, cracked, and all-hope-shattering egg.
He couldn't nick. He went unbreakfasted
in a quiet room of feasible breakfasts.

There was a silver lining. There were some
seventy-five teabags he could use.
He used one, took it black, and used the lemon.

'I'm having lemon tea,' he said, truly.
'It's no bad thing sometimes to go hungry.'
'Bollocks,' said his stomach, a young Tory.

He re-opened his magazine. So many
adverts nowadays, hardly a page
of honest information, he was thinking,

turning the pages. Then he heard a sound
upstairs, thought something of it, then sat back.
Gave a sigh, decided to go out.

VI

It ought to have been gathered: it was hot.
The children's eggs were softening or gone
and the parents? merely coping, as they'd done

a thousand times before. More than that.
The last corner shop was cool, though, all
the goods were cool and sound, the sell-by dates

were up ahead – perilous sell-by dates!
No one underestimates them now,
not since the old lady died in Glossop.

The owner of the shop, the girl's father,
was puzzled. He was in the shop himself:
'These eggs, so very popular...' he mused.

His daughter humbly nodded: 'All this morning,
everyone.' 'I cannot understand,'
the owner said. (He'd try one, later on,

throw most of it away, and remain puzzled.
She, however, nodding now, in fact
had eaten one, and hidden one.) They shrugged.

The sun inched on to N and it was noon.
The skinhead rose and recognised the head
of Clare, his ex, her hair extremely red,

her bangled hands haggling over bangles.
'Oi, sweet'art!' he shouted in the sun.
Not nobody's sweetheart, she carried on.

VII

And out into the day ambled the one
unbreakfasted and eager citizen
yet to see what new thing had been done.

The brown-haired bloke saw children seeing it,
he saw their parent(s) seeing it and groaning,
he saw hot drivers bored and interested.

Then he saw it. A vast advertisement
for chocolate eggs. It was a chocolate egg,
or paper reproduction, but enormous.

There was no slogan. That did strike him then –
the sheer nerve, the worthless new idea!
Filling up that gap on that old building!

He'd stopped by now, the bloke. He also thought
it did resemble something not an egg.
Something lazing in a rich man's bed,

something bald and powerful, perhaps
a general. He scoffed at it, and walked
(thinking of the immorality,

100

the trivial creativity, the waste!)
straight into the skinhead. 'Fuckin'ell!
Watch it, mate...Oi, sweet'art, wait for me!'

The hungry bloke, forgotten, rubbed his head.
Blinked in the exacting sunlight, stood
pondering in his rough neighbourhood.

VIII

For he was the next customer. His feet
were inches from the nearest corner shop.
He looked relieved, and jangled through the door.

The door jingled behind him. He was in
and choosing bacon, bread, some apple juice
if possible, and being shown it was:

the Indian girl was pleased to see his hair.
In the dark behind her loomed her father,
worriedly stocktaking in the corner.

The brown-haired bloke got ready with his choices:
bacon, bread, milk, apple juice. He checked
a scribbled list, and mentioned eggs aloud.

The father froze. The girl looked in the box
marked CHOCOLATE EGGS, and saw how few there were.
Four: there'd been a run. She reached for the box.

'God, not those things,' chuckled the customer,
always right, and looking in the box,
'The ones that come from farmers!' He bought six.

A satisfying customer, he left,
mulling over possibilities:
a bacon sandwich, poach the eggs perhaps.

Tea with milk, but in which cup? The brown?
Yes, call it a brunch. The bloke looked up.
Clouding over now. 'In the brown cup.'

IX

The afternoon, some three hours after noon,
not unlike the marketplace, began
to let in gaps and sighs of weariness.

Women stretched, men bent down to lift.
Karen, Clare, and Karen from the hat-stall
made their way towards a corner shop,

via the long pavement over which
the cloud-darkened egg presided, big.
They chatted as girls do, as some girls do,

they jingled in, acknowledged by the owner,
who'd let his daughter out to buy a fish.
They made a lot of noise, and what they bought

is not important. What they didn't, is:
a chocolate egg. They bought three, certainly,
but left a single one. Just 30p!

You'd think they'd go the whole hog, wouldn't you?
Instead they left, chatting as some girls do.
The door jangled behind them. In the shop,

a good man's consternation at supply
almost dry, demand still running high:
he glared at the chocolate egg...But outside, this:

'Sweet'art, wait for me! I wanna talk!'
The skinhead chased his ex down Bootlace Street.
The Karens shrieked, began to overeat.

   X

Digesting on his own, in a dull room,
checking on the fixtures, switching on
the small colour television, seeing

various ridiculous programmes, each
greeted with a groan and some attention,
some twenty seconds till another change,

from all the matches after half-an-hour
strangely at 0–0, (on ORACLE)
to tribesmen fishing things on Channel 4,

to endless steeplechasing in the rain
at Haydock Park and Doncaster and Welshmen
coming sixty-fourth in a downpour,

102

to that same and increasingly bizarre
black-and-white from 1944,
in which the Colonel opens the wrong door

and reads the latest scores – to CEEFAX now,
where most games were 1–1, and the good news
on the news-sheet, 102, the crash,

was that the firemen, ambulancemen, guardsmen,
policemen, passers-by, ringmasters, kids,
backwoodsmen, poets, acrobats, and thieves

had done a marvellous job, and the death-toll
was falling rapidly, and Heads of State
were representing us by being there

XI

a while after the dying, – and changing back
to final betting on the 4.15,
the Colonel saying 'I don't know what you mean!'

the tribesmen being interviewed, the match
at Alloa abandoned, and the race
won convincingly by seven Kenyans,

and lunch's rumble settled, the sound upstairs
of Oliver, inching towards the shower,
and all our Saturdays the usual, he,

the brown-haired bloke, he – anyway, he sighed.
'Rubbish,' he said, switched to another side
he didn't know existed. It was new.

Its name was STAR, (Lindsay must've
fixed it up, a dish outside?) it showed
seven different programmes: at that instant

Cul-de-Sac was on, an episode
the brown-haired bloke had never seen, in which
Flinzi, the success-story, was sad.

She wasn't getting on with her real dad.
Her former dad was smiling just behind her.
She cried all the way to the commercials.

The bloke was laughing 'Ha! It's rubbish! Ha!'
Rather loudly, everything else was quiet.
Then came this particular commercial.

XII

o. A brown *o*, starting rather small.
(Hell, you know what's coming, but he didn't.)
A bigger, browner, chocolatier *O*

impossible to demonstrate, but there
on its silk background lay the one
unannotated, unexplained, unsold

egg of earlier. There was no slogan.
There *was* music, either by Johnny Cash,
the Beatles or the Everlys, whoever,

but not a word was spoken. By the end,
by the thirtieth second, the whole screen
was brown and cream-filled. Then, on white, the words

CUL-DE-SAC. For rather a long time.
Then Shane accusing Laurel, Laurel hurt,
Stacy curious, Roger on the prowl,

and Flinzi bravely smiling through. Through what?
The television wasn't on. These things
occurred elsewhere. I don't know where. The room

was empty, and the front door lightly shut.
Nothing happened here, unless you count
Oliver's bedraggledly appearing,

eating Lindsay's bacon, someone's eggs,
someone's croissant, settling down to watch
the end of *CUL-DE-SAC*. Someone got shot.

XIII

'Just the one,' the bloke was thinking, 'Just
to try, it's bound to be disgusting, just
to experience a culinary low...'

He crossed at the pedestrian crossing,
ahead of the pedestrians, it seemed
to him they heard him, censured him for thinking

'culinary' – probably they'd laugh
to see him clip the kerb! Serve 'im right!
they'd think – he thought, he did, and then they did:

'Enjoy yer trip?' laughed someone in a fez.
'But is it hunger?' was a later thought,
while walking by the finished marketplace,

'or merely greed?' 'It's greed,' said half of him,
the upper half; 'It's hunger,' went the rest,
all accomplished liars there, but charmers.

There was the advertisement, the hoarding!
A great, swollen full-stop on his hopes
of backing out, and the silk made it worse:

The bloke was going to eat the chocolate egg!
There it was, in brown-and-purple! Big!
There was the corner shop! In which he'd even

said he didn't want to, and meant it!
What would they think of him – Avid, pale,
returning, with a brown look in his eye?

XIV

'In the extraordinary, implausible
but nonetheless respected – if bizarre –
event of your not being totally

and utterly, completely, creamily,
dreamily, creme-fondant centrally
satisfied, delighted, nay, amazed,

converted, charmed and spellbound by our product,
– strange, somewhat perverse as such dissent
may seem to decent, civilised consumers –

you may of course tell us precisely what
has worried you, disturbed you in your great
cloud-cadbury-land of culinary nous,

and even tell us where you deigned to purchase
such unpleasing fare, and roughly when
you thought you'd stretch to 30p for this

Cadillac of Chocolates – thank you so much! –
we'd obviously bend arse over tit
accommodating you, mighty one:

just tell us who could do with some cheap chocs,
and where they live. We'll send our Family Box.'
'Nutrition Information. Every egg

contains 8g Fat, 1.7 Protein,
Carbohydrate 26.5.'
ROLAND RAT SAYS KEEP YOUR COUNTRY CLEAN.

XV

The brown-haired bloke was at the door. He had
a hot pound coin in his hand, his face
expressed a wish to be expressionless,

and he was in the shop. The aisles were narrow,
the place was empty, but for the quiet mother
gazing past the bloke at the canned soups,

then he was at the counter. There was a box,
being somewhat profligate with the facts:
CHOCOLATE EGGS – a bald untruthful plural.

The bloke observed the egg in all its smallness.
Its wrapper was all shiny reds and golds,
unlike the brazen nude advertisement –

which hadn't been a factor, he assured
his upper house of cerebral detractors,
all whistling him to pay his stupid coin

and live with it. He opened his whole mouth
as someone charged into the shop, the door
jingling apologetically behind –

'Gimme a half o'Teachers, sweet'art! Oi,
you again! Outta me way, I'm first!
An' I'll 'ave that chocko egg an'all, sweet'art!

Me fuckin' sweet'art's buggered off, sweet'art!
'ere – 'ave a fiver, that'll do it. Oi,
watch it, matey! Ta-ra, Gunga Din!'

106

XVI

He jangled out. The daughter jingled in,
without a fish, but telling her mother why
in Urdu. As for the next customer,

he bought a TIME, with the planet on its front.
Then he left, now really hungry.
A sad agreement of his bickering halves.

The shopkeepers had looked at him strangely.
Then talked in their language. The girl moved
over to the counter, where the box

boasting CHOCOLATE EGGS was a brown lie.
She picked it up and said some more. Her mother
made a sign of resignation, almost

philosophical, then turned away,
back into the rooms behind, talking.
The daughter heard the radio go on,

heard of the shock-result in Liverpool,
the muddy draw in Middlesbrough, the old
world-record broken by a man called Ngu,

the amazing binding packs of the All-Blacks
and gallant British losses everywhere.
And she didn't understand, and didn't care.

The day's last customers were from the States.
They were lost. 'We're looking for the East?'
'You are here,' the Indian told them. They weren't pleased.

XVII

In the Dog and Barrow, Clare the Ex-
Girlfriend of the Skinhead sipped her half
and gained the weight she'd lost escaping him.

Karen, Karen from the hat-stall, Wayne,
Bruno, Debs and Shaz from the Arndale
began three conversations, one on clothes,

one on that 1–1 draw at Anfield, one
on that same skinhead standing by the door
watching them, filling his beer-glass

with shots of Teachers whisky. 'Well I'm firsty,'
he told the nearest codger, who was deaf
and hadn't asked. It must have been 'round six.

It was just then the Americans came in,
ordering what couldn't be provided.
Angry that it couldn't be provided.

'We'll sort 'im out,' said Wayne, at the table.
'If he comes near you –' Bruno said. 'He will,'
said Karen from the hat-stall, quite excited:

'He did this afternoon! She had to peg it!'
'Yeah,' said Clare, 'No fanks to you.' 'What for?'
the blonder Karen shrieked: 'He ain't *our* boyfriend!'

Not no one's boyfriend, overhearing all,
the skinhead scratched his head and made a plan.
'I'll sort 'er out,' he told a passing man.

XVIII

A cool and clouded dusk was coming on.
The sun had gone to pieces long before,
and one or two had felt drops on the wind.

The brown-haired bloke had walked a half-mile west
in search of other corner shops. He'd passed
burger-houses, hair-salons, bookies,

estate agents, and video rental shops,
but nothing quite like what he needed. Or,
wanted. He was past the needing stage,

really he was just walking a new way,
he didn't know the area at all.
He wanted to get something from today.

But most things were closed, and he began,
very gradually, to change his thinking
on this especial want, this chocolate egg.

– 'This chocolate egg'! Ha! A lucky escape!
Thank God for skinheads! – those kinds of thoughts,
compensations, lonely, in the street.

Of course, the problem with a half-mile walk
is that it takes a half to make it home,
to make a mile. He sighed, and turned a U.

Perhaps it was time to put that treat behind him,
to concentrate on proper evening food,
something good-for-you, something good.

XIX

Well hell – it happened so fast – where do you start?
Let's see what people said, then what they did
when the unpleasantness occurred that recent

Saturday – Wayne said they'd 'sort 'im out';
Bruno concurred in that – instead they sat
speechless, motionless, as he strode through

the crowded Dog and Barrow – the skinhead –
wielding something small and probably
vicious – but they sat and stared at him,

and the girls saw him late, his ex was last
of all to see the start of a long arc,
his armed hand scything through the smoke

to land, a bird, in her red spiky nest
with an endangering squelch: and to recede,
leaving its botch of brown, yellow, white,

egg-resemblers melted to the facts –
Protein, Carbohydrate, mostly Fat –
sticky highlights in a shock of hair.

The skinhead backed away, his hand a mess,
but somehow a successful mess, and anyway,
he wiped it on the codger's head. The boys

were on their feet, but powerless to piece
the chocolate into egg. 'I love yer, Clare,'
the skinhead hoarsely cried. 'Fuck off,' said Clare,

XX

watching him leave the pub, and in fact her life.
But bashing into someone's yet again –
the homecoming and optimistic bloke,

TIME in hand, an evening meal to make,
a friend to find, perhaps a girl – but no,
a burping skinhead telling him where to go,

telling him where to put it, telling him 'Oh,
I love 'er, she's my girl!' and vanishing
lurching down an alley, and then quiet.

And then a stranger crossing the quiet street
towards him, a girl, nobody he knew.
He looked behind him, trying to work out who

it was she was approaching. It was him.
'I'm hiding it,' she said, in her disguise.
She gave it to him, looked into his eyes,

brown as hers, but no one said a thing,
and two moments too many passed: she turned
and hurried off. He opened his right hand:

golds and reds in the streetlight – the last
unconsumed and still-desired delight...
The bloke looked up, the girl dodged out of sight,

but followed him until he closed his door,
still very puzzled. Then she hurried home.
The bloke began unwrapping in his room.

XXI

O Egg, your garments are of gold and scarlet!
Egg, you have that brown aroma! Egg,
you look so small but you can fill all holes!

But I don't need to eat you! You have nothing
my body needs, you may do lasting harm!
You cost too much, you're fattening! You're mine!

Outside on Meat Street, where the Market was,
the awnings flapped, the rain quickly began,
the advertising hoardings wrinkled. One,

the largest-ever, the one for Chocolate Eggs,
was such a vast expanse of paper, the rain
overweighted it. An upper corner

110

peeled from the wall, and the rainwater
sliced behind the sheet, bringing it down
slowly, magisterially, to earth

to swamp the market-stalls, a white tarpaulin.
The first twelve men to notice this rushed on
regardless, but a thirteenth phoned his boss

who carried on as normal, in his bath.
Night fell. Put it another way: England
spun out into darkness, didn't count,

didn't have the sun, had all the rest.
What else? The bloke, (my hero, I admit)
scoffed the thing and didn't die of it.

Farm Close

The small field by my house is the small field
I mean: the old green field of incidents,
small teams, comments, and the planned insult.

It's just the same to look at, like my book
with the Straw-Witch on page 9, the frightener!
It doesn't frighten me, but nothing does.

On the small field now, different goalkeepers
minding their own when the quarrel starts
and different bullies asking, but still doomed

to weeks in jail or profits in South London.
Different targets too, but they deserve it,
and I feel towards them like the ones we had.

Just drab men punching in the rain.
For me to stop them, stop the usual hurt,
would be to disrupt the business of a town,

or change the future of a small, determined planet.
And I'm just the mad beloved Time-Traveller
who, as you probably know, can't do that.